## ABOUT KEY TO THE HIGHWAY

When you think you know where you are in a Chris Hardy poem, look again, because the ground is uncertain and there is a growing sense of unease that the time for leisurely reading may run out before he writes the last line, or the calendar rips out its pages. These are poems with an eye on fable, desert snakes, privet hedges and an ear for the music words make in the quiet of a page. *The Key to the Highway* is yours for the taking, so adventure away! But, 'Only later can you make out/how it all went together,/that what you saw passed through you/like a spear of light.'

– Helen Ivory

# KEY TO THE HIGHWAY

# PREVIOUS BOOKS BY CHRIS HARDY

*Buddha* – 1984, Holt, Rinehart and Wilson

*Swimming In The Deep Diamond Mine* – 2002, Hub Editions

*A Moment Of Attention* – 2008, Original Plus

*Write Me A Few Of Your Lines* – 2012, Graft Poetry

*Sunshine At The End Of The World* – 2017, Indigo Dreams Publishing

# KEY TO THE HIGHWAY

## CHRIS HARDY

*I've got the key to the highway,
I'm billed out and bound to go,
I'm going to leave here running because
walking's much too slow.*

'Key To The Highway'
– Big Bill Broonzy

All rights reserved. No part of this work covered by the copyright herein may be reproduced or used in any means – graphic, electronic, or mechanical, including copying, recording, taping, or information storage and retrieval systems – without written permission of the publisher.

Printed by imprintdigital
Upton Pyne, Exeter
www.digital.imprint.co.uk

Typesetting and cover design by The Book Typesetters
us@thebooktypesetters.com
07422 598 168
www.thebooktypesetters.com

Published by Shoestring Press
19 Devonshire Avenue, Beeston, Nottingham, NG9 1BS
(0115) 925 1827
www.shoestringpress.co.uk

First published 2021
© Copyright: Chris Hardy
© Cover painting: Martha Hardy

The moral right of the author has been asserted.

ISBN 978-1-912524-81-5

# ACKNOWLEDGEMENTS

My thanks to the members of the Barnes and Chichester stanzas, and Red Door Poets, and the editors of the following publications and websites where some of the poems in this book have appeared:

1handclapping.online
Acumen
algebraofowls.com
As Above So Below
atriumpoetry.com
Chichester festival open mic poems 2020
clearpoetry.wordpress.com
Confluence
Dempsey & Windle publishing
Dreamcatcher
ekphrastic.net
Fire
Frogmore Papers
inksweatandtears.co.uk
Lampeter Review
londongrip.co.uk
maryevans.com
ninemusespoetry.com
Oasis
Obsessed With Pipework
odyssey.pm
Orbis
peacockjournal.com
Pennine Platform
picaroonpoetry.wordpress.com
Poetry Birmingham Literary Journal
Poetry & All That Jazz
Poetry Salzburg Review
Presence
Raceme
riggwelterpress.wordpress.com
South
South Bank Poetry
Stand
the Alchemy Spoon
the Blue Nib
the Frogmore Papers
the High Window
thehighwindowpress.com
the Journal
thelakepoetry.co.uk
the North
thepoetryvillage.com
wordsforthewild.co.uk
writingatthebeachhut.org

'Key to the highway' was commended in the Canterbury poet of the year competition 2017 and published in the anthology.

'Solstice' was commended in the Barnet open poetry competition 2019 and published in the anthology.

'Jacob' came second in the Guernsey Poetry Festival's 'Poetry On The Move' competition 2019 and was displayed on the island's buses and aeroplanes.

'Kirpan' and 'Cleaning Up' were shortlisted for the Welshpool Poetry Festival competition 2019.

'Verona' was commended in the Shoreham Words Festival 2020 and published in the anthology.

For Roger, Steve and Walter

# CONTENTS

| | |
|---|---|
| Number One | 1 |
| Naming Rain | 2 |
| Tempo | 3 |
| Whitsun in Blackpool | 4 |
| Catching Silver | 6 |
| Permanganate | 7 |
| Lord Dismiss Us | 8 |
| Banquet | 9 |
| Key to the Highway | 10 |
| Hesperides | 12 |
| Crossing the Threshold | 14 |
| Cleaning up | 15 |
| Each Summer | 16 |
| Listen Silent | 17 |
| Dragon's Tail | 18 |
| Professional | 20 |
| Behind the Sun | 22 |
| Sound Is Slow Light Is Quick | 23 |
| Knock Knock | 24 |
| And Four Types of Hornbill | 26 |
| Eden | 28 |
| Giblet | 31 |
| Golgotha | 32 |
| Earth Rise July 20th 1969 | 34 |
| Defeat | 35 |
| This Is Why | 36 |
| War Paint | 37 |

| | |
|---|---|
| Fighting Chance | 38 |
| Asosa | 39 |
| Sandy Pylos | 40 |
| A Matter of Course | 42 |
| All the Numbered Years | 43 |
| Solstice | 44 |
| Near Clun | 46 |
| House Hunting | 48 |
| A Stop on the Way | 50 |
| I Never Thought I'd Live Round Here so Long | 51 |
| Holding the Line | 52 |
| Some Enchanted Evening | 54 |
| Against England | 56 |
| Eastern and Oriental | 58 |
| Verona | 59 |
| The Wind Forgets, Always Forgets | 60 |
| In Sure and Certain Hope | 62 |
| Give Us This Day March 29th 2020 | 65 |
| Forecasting the Present | 66 |
| Also | 68 |
| The Bridge | 69 |
| Leaving Now | 70 |
| Jacob | 72 |
| Midwinter Invitation | 73 |
| When It's All Said and Done | 74 |
| Did You Make It? | 76 |

# NUMBER ONE

She wore a flowered dress
and the Autumn sun
came through the glass
so light chalk dust
was a mist between me,
the window and the path
to the churchyard where
in a flint wall
coins were left
for me to find.

Was it the first day?
We copied numbers
from the board.
2 was a shape
I could not draw.
She wrote it for me
in my book.
I copied 1 down easily
and later saw
that 1 was also I.

In the picture of the class
we are looking at the lens
which looks straight back
as it buries us alive.

# NAMING RAIN

We can walk, then climb that last bit.
Orchids fill the meadows.
I am breathless at the top,
though it is not high,
but recover instantly.
The plain is green, purple,
yellow, white,
beneath a hurrying sky.

I have a name for this place,
and know where the wind,
scattering drops of rain
with a red speck of sand
inside each, like an ant
in amber on my shoes,
comes from. Somewhere else
in this world.

# TEMPO

In Mr Montano's room
I learned the violin.

Holding the bow
press taut hair
against the string.

The sound should be
mahogany.
My mother hears the tune

chase my eyes
across the staves
as she waits outside.

I left the quavers
in the air,
like dust or seconds

or the silent tick
of an unwound clock
when the door is locked

and Mr Montano
takes tea and beef kailan
at the tennis club.

The ball skims
back and forth
across the net,

thock thock
thock.

# WHITSUN IN BLACKPOOL

Oz came back from driving tanks
across the Mareth line,
to walk six miles a day along
a battery of chattering looms.

Muriel waited without leave or letter,
sometimes a card with a tick against
'I am well' – 'I am in hospital'.
In that time she lost her youth
and found confectionery instead.

The Rover ticks outside
at four o'clock on Sunday.
Shop door locked, shutters down
on shelves of blackjacks,
pear drops, sherbet dip.

Hot tea cooling in a saucer,
soft ginger cake with butter,
cheese, white bread, sliced onion.
A square of Nottingham lace
upon the locked piano lid.

In coal-dust scented fog
John and Trevor clump
the sodden leather pill,
sing, *You, me and uz,
we are my favourite people.*

A flying saucer topped
with a vast typewriter
surfaces in the Tower ballroom.
Gasps of melancholy blow
across the empty auditorium.

The morning train took me away.
How do we arrive if
we don't know where we're going?
Oz knew what must happen,
he'd seen enough in Egypt,

but didn't waste a minute
on how or when and yet it came,
a sentence from his son.
The one who went to Canada
for a year's work, found a girl,

travelled west to the Pacific,
spread before his window,
such a sight, unthought of
never dreamt
that long weekend in England.

# CATCHING SILVER

Three ships outside the harbour,
two destroyers and a liner,
and my mother asking,
*Who gives way?*

Boys in the water
beneath the bow,
swimming among pipe fish
and spidery, green medusas,

shouting up for money,
catching specks of silver
that flash down in the sun,
in their mouths.

Men lying by the road
I thought were dead
but were asleep,
dozens of them,

and children who followed
with imploring hands,
shouting and fighting
when I dropped some coins.

Only later can you make out
how it all went together,
that what you saw passed through you
like a spear of light.

# PERMANGANATE

I made a road for my toy cars
along a bank beneath the peach trees
while a red animal ran in the wood.

The wood was dark green,
entered by stepping over a ditch
one mattock blade wide,
cut to irrigate the garden.

We scooped water from the furrow
to uncouple a dog and bitch
stuck snapping, screaming.

If blocked the stream became
a pool until the gardener
broke my wall with his foot.

Once we threw rocks at the neighbours
then ran and as I slammed the door
stones battered against it.

My mother covered her face
with hands stained purple because
sweet fruit might kill us all.

The door was blue,
I don't know why,
but everything was painted
by itself.

From the sack of puppies
in the boot of the car
I kept one.

# LORD DISMISS US

Where are you my friends,
have you survived the years
of diaries, rents, the morning
and the evening key,
entering and leaving
all the days that appear
outside the door?

And why do I
this afternoon recall
when we were last together?
Teachers bidding us
good luck, farewell,

then on the train,
our bags in racks,
we threw our blue caps
lined with red
from the windows and
they hung in the trees
like birds.

# BANQUET

Clouds of scented dust drop
from the iron-wood tiles of the club.
A buffet of chicken, egg, potato curry,
rice, chopped banana, coconut,
diced chilli.

My father at the bar,
holding a tin of fifty
Navy Cut.
My mother by the window,
a hand of bridge,
iced Gin-and-It.

In the pool we display.
You wrestle him while she
hands off her rival,
rides your neck,
long deafening legs
clutch your ears.

We cannot eat or drink,
lying on the bank's
sharp grass,
simmering with
centipedes and ants.

The tree snake looped
in the bougainvillea
is unafraid of us,
who like her
firm green coils,
her soft black fork.

# KEY TO THE HIGHWAY
*Big Bill Broonzy, Copenhagen, 1956.*

I spent years trying to learn
how you made the shuffle
and the tune roll out together
while sliding the strings about
on the fretboard as if your guitar
was as easy to handle
as a slack clothes line.

Clouds of smoke,
glasses clink,
you pause to swallow
cough and joke

with suited Danes
who laugh
and then sit silent
when they hear,

*If you's white it's alright,*
*if you's brown stick around,*
*but as you's black O brother,*
*get back get back get back.*

That last session
before your voice gave out,
you carried the jumbo to the chair
with a big fist round its throat,
trusting your thumb would still find C,
your fingers G and E
and the hole in the soundboard
into which guitarists never look

would testify again
what words can only say,
the long beat loose
inside a handmade chord,
which unlocked the door
to the highway that began
outside my mother's house.

# HESPERIDES

After driving across Spain
we got lost in the desert.
Came to a white
and brown tower,
went through the door,
climbed the stairs
and there,
in the air and light
from open windows,
met for the first time
those who only wear
stockings.

Their smiles made us run.
Soon after my friend
was on his knees
in a hospital
where they gave us
the only cold water
in the country.

I do not mean
that what happened
at the tower
made him sick.
I mean I remember
the women who smiled
and were unafraid,
knew everything
when we knew nothing,
not even where we were
or how we'd got there.

The desert was not yellow
but red and black.
That too
was unexpected.
You can learn a little
if you pay attention.
Cold water heals
like a smile.
Your maps are wrong.

# CROSSING THE THRESHOLD

How hot it was that summer,
blue exhaust dust seeping in
between shut, rattling sashes,
taxis and buses shuddering
toward Hammersmith
outside our window.

The ground floor room
by the front door that was
never locked, sometimes not shut,
was the only one unlet.
Boots stamped lino day and night,
stumbling in the dark
or stumbling drunk.

When we were out, looking for work,
signing on, or at the registry office
booking our slot, they broke in,
took all we had worth anything -
my good guitar, our passports
and the wedding ring you didn't wear
because we were not wed.

Standing in the room,
the splintered door behind me
swinging loose,
London hammering down the hall,
I knew without looking
what we were missing.

# CLEANING UP

When short you could always get work
for a cleaning agency,
and be paid cash across a plywood desk
in a small, neon-lit office
somewhere off the Balls Pond Road.

I was sent to knock on the doors
of double fronted villas
in Chalk Farm and Belsize Park,
with metal window frames,
fitted beige carpets
and glass topped coffee tables.

The housewives took one look at me
on the step and instantly knew
I was not a habitual or
effective cleaner of houses.

But they let me in,
handed over mop, bucket, brush and pan,
dusters, polish and the vacuum cleaner
all of which, in random and haphazard fashion
I would immediately deploy.

Once I'd made a start and
they'd returned to their Canasta,
tea and biscuits, Silk Cut King Size
on the go all afternoon,
I'd leave the vacuum droning noisily
and search the cupboards for gin.

Though I was handsome then
and young, I was never propositioned
which, looking back on it,
seems a shame.

# EACH SUMMER

Fourty pounds for the Summer.
Jed took the big window out
and banged a frame and casement
into the hole like a missing tooth
he'd made in the white wall.

We fitted a new window to leave it open
and let everything that was out there,
moths, cats, ants, beetles, rain,
come in, if it wanted to.

And gourds of scented air
that emptied in the rooms,
filling the house with
sleeping fields and hedgerows.

Each morning a nest of ash
shivered in the grate as a breeze
like water round our feet found its way
from the window to the chimney.

Then we mended brickwork,
roof and doors but kept the falling barn
of dried out planks wavering upright
in the wind and dust,
where swallows lived each Summer.

# LISTEN
# SILENT

Everyone round here's asleep
also dogs birds foxes cats.
The wind has dropped
and the fridge is off.

Aircraft are landing
somewhere else and
no one is driving down my street.
No one doesn't exist.

My house is old
and settles on itself
peacefully as if
after a large meal.

I listen to silence
and hear it all.

I also hear myself
hissing like a fountain
in a dawn piazza.
Bronze dolphins

arch their backs
as the sun
reaching out
from side streets

opens windows
in wet paving,
before people wake
and buses run.

# DRAGON'S TAIL

In October lay the hedge.
Keep hawthorn, hazel,
blackthorn, beech and ash.
Behead the oak.

Slice stems to a tendon
of sapwood with the hook.
Pack down the pleachers at a slant,
staked with poles, bound by whips.

Haul away everything cut out –
long twisted branches, brash,
axed trunks, young growth, dead wood,
and stack it in the field.

Fire will change it to
a hill of incandescent caves
from which a ring of flame
will spread across dry stubble.

You're left with a barrier
dense and sharp, chest high,
a straight dark line
leaning up the slope,

and a circle of black earth
where nothing grows
until April rain wakes
thistle seeds blown in.

Soon cornflowers, hare bells,
orchids, vetch and grass return,
are mown, raked out to dry,
baled in stacks and barns,

like gold sieved from the earth
for feed when fields are bare,
when waterfalls of stars
fall through the skylight,

and the hedge is sinew, ribcage,
spine of the sleeping serpent
round your bounds
that you laid there.

# PROFESSIONAL

After the interview,
where I could see the sky
behind my questioner's
tired face,

I was appointed,
despite my jacket
that smelled
of the sausage factory.

A degree was all
that was required
to teach the children
of the Harrow Road.

The Head was furious
when I walked in at 11 am
sure I wouldn't have to work
on day one.

On the way upstairs
I saw a man throwing kids
back through a door
as they ran out.

It seemed a sort of game
they'd agreed to play.
Later he told me
he was moving to Bodmin.

In the classroom
the girls sat patiently
in the front row
while I grabbed the ball

to stop a match being played
behind the desks.
With a piece of chalk
I wrote the date

on the board and said
*write that down.*
They did.
We began our education.

# BEHIND THE SUN

I went to the trees to collect
knot-holed spars lying in the snow,
brought down by the heavy fall piled
in glistening slices along their boughs.

Cut branches to red heartwood,
barrowed a full load to the barn,
built a cord, racked and stowed,
four by eight by four.

What's done is done for all of us
there that night, watching larch
in the burning cradle spit and flare,
hoping to get away, drive east at dawn

to where what we became was waiting,
our children kneeling on the seat
looking back, their lives pouring in
through the windscreen behind them.

# SOUND IS SLOW LIGHT IS QUICK

The day I came of age
was later than
it happens now.
With some others
I lay on the floor
in the dark because
night then began
in the afternoon.

A stack of vinyl
on the turntable.
One disc drops
with a soft tap,
the tone arm clicks,
needle hiss,
Revolver, Dylan,
I forget the rest.

That was how winter
went away, leaving only music.
Then I stood up and
pressed a switch
so when I left
I could look back
and see a window flare
in the distance.

# KNOCK KNOCK

I'm here
where you will be

I'm not a ghost
I pay cash

my foot hurts
in the morning

when I get in my car
I think of death.

*

We found a ring
on the ground

and got married
to comfort the landlord

if this tap drips
for a thousand years

the sink
will wear away.

*

There's a million people
floating

in this city
suspended

in its rooms
after a while

the mark on the wall
is painted over.

\*

When he threw
a paper plane

from a window
that circled

down to land
on grass

I knew
I was going to die.

\*

Wake silent morning,
hear what's outside

and between the stars.
Silent as the grave

is wrong only life
can be silent

a knock on the door
of an empty room.

# AND FOUR TYPES OF HORNBILL

I saw all these and many more,
wrote down the names
they did not know,
marks on paper not in air.
Tiny spirits which dwell in sky,
pick specks from earth
enough to fly.

\*

Red Faced Collybird
Lazy Grass Warbler
Indian Swift

Yellow Backed Widowbird
Lilac Breasted Roller
Horus Swift

Cabani's Weaverbird
Blue Cheeked Bee Eater
Yellow Throated Long Claw

Kirk's Black Sunbird
Black Capped Tchagra
Monteiro's Mosque Swallow

Malachite Sunbird
Pallid Harrier
Meechow's Chanting Goshawk

Yellow Bishopbird
Nyasa Seed Cracker
Ngami Bourbon Shrike

Pin Tailed Widowbird
Raquet Tailed Roller
White Browed Coucal

and four types,
Trumpeter, Red Billed,
Crowned and Grey,
of Hornbill.

\*

My mother told the priest
to say my name out loud.
I did not choose,
or ask *why this?*
and now it is too late,
but people know me by it,
like a bird.

# EDEN

Though I have lived in jungle and savannah
I am not much acquainted with snakes.

\*

Fallen from the roof of the balcony
the dozing nāgā lies upon the shoulder
of a woman dining in the evening air.

When a bowl of milk is placed before it
the snake slips onto the table where a bullet
destroys the hamadryad and the table.

\*

Pointing to the pale-beaked sea snake
struggling in grey waves off the esplanade
my father tells me it is poisonous,

as all serpents are that live in the sea.
Two brown nerofithi idling by a pond
are looking for frogs not me.

\*

Though I have lived in jungle and savannah
I am not much acquainted with snakes.
Now I live in a northern city where they don't live.

\*

I captured a grass snake with a tented book.
Left it to starve when the holidays began.
Returned to rings in a see-through sock.

My mother stopped me picking up
a lurid pencil from the ground
by pointing out a dragon on a twig.

Resting in a storm drain the viper
hears me on the bridge above and slides away.
Its scales scratch the concrete like dry leaves.

Thick bodied adder looped on a rock,
a golden rope that licks the air
when I come across her in the heather.

\*

Though I have lived in jungle and savannah
I am not much acquainted with snakes.
Now I live in a northern city
which edges out into fields
where they don't live.

\*

My neighbour killed a fira in his bathroom.
Next night its mate was waiting so
he blew cobra and bath to bits with a shotgun.

I met him again in Wales in '76,
and after agreeing the burnt hillsides
smelt of Africa we recognised each other.

\*

A bootlace coiled beneath the doorstep
the spitofithi hisses like a cat
as with a broom I encourage it to leave.

In the middle of the road above the port
an old man curses the small whip snake
he is beating to death with a stick.

\*

Though I have lived in jungle and savannah
I am not much acquainted with snakes.
Now I live in a northern city
which edges out into fields
which edge out into forest
where they don't live.

*nāgā* – snake (Hindi)
*hamadryad* – king cobra (Hindi)
*nerofithi* – water snake (Greek)
*fira* – cobra (Swahili)
*spitofithi* – house snake (Greek)

# GIBLET

A sparrow hawk
has pinned a starling
on its back, wings spread
on my soft lawn.

The starling is alive
and strains its head
to watch the hawk
tear out feathers,

skin, heart and lungs
on a string.
I do not interfere.
We are superior to a hawk.

When we do the same
we know what we are doing.

# GOLGOTHA

Vultures circle above the city
on Good Friday.
Trucks of sheep and chickens
pull up outside the market.
Oxen stumble from the pavement
into traffic, compelled
by a buffalo whip.

Bulls and lambs hobbled in alleys.
Hot afternoon, the day moves slow.
In yards and kitchens animals shift,
heads bowed in the silence.
Mallets, knives, concealed, to hand.

Churches stacked with silent drums.
We buy a rooster, pulled
from the fluttering tangle
on a flat-bed trailer.
Red wattles and wings flap loose
as we carry it, hanging
from bound feet.

Christ's sacrifice acclaimed -
stand, bow, fall, rise,
stand, bow, fall down, all night -
then go to clashing chambers,
greased hands shine
in smoke-dim light.
Yellow sand turns red then black.

Sixty days of fasting bought
with piles of bone and slithered bowel,
for rats, pi-dogs and the poor
to suck on once the vultures
have had their fill, snake necks
stretched up, heads back, beaks ajar,
drinking guts like water.

The skin man collects hides
and dries them on thorn brake,
spread to stab scavengers in the eye
and stop them getting at
the donkey's cross-striped foal.

Horned gods line the kerb
until hyenas come, gibbering,
gulping skulls and pulp,
leave chalk-dry shit
the farmer's plough folds into
soft black earth for cotton,
winter shawls against the cold.

# EARTH RISE JULY 20TH 1969

We sat beside the estuary
throwing pebbles in the air,

small brown planets
against the soft blue sky.

That day I dropped my watch
into a well saying,

*I'm done with time*
and the water far below agreed.

In a corner of the front room
grey, white, black shades moved

upon a small, impossible stage.
We caught a mermaid in a net

and didn't kill her.
If we can do that

with everyone watching
we are clear and free.

It's midsummer,
winter will not come this year,
maybe never.

# DEFEAT

French coins showered from a train
stopped on the bridge over Latchmere Road.
Tired soldiers emptying their pockets
of change, lightening the load.

Their pale, fag-hanging faces
grinned down at us scrabbling after
silver bouncing in the gutter,
which we could not count or use.

Brambles in the lane are
heavy with fruit this year.
Black and sweet from Summer rain,
and before that heat. Weather
to make the grass grow quick
so it must be cut, and cut again.

# THIS IS WHY
*With thanks to my mother who told me.*

We saw a small flower open
from a black-red burst
in the sky, clear and blue,
traced with thin white threads.
Our teacher let us and we ran
with cooks and kitchen girls
across the fields,
reached him as he tried to rise,
tangled in rope twisted round
his blue-grey blouse,
struggling to pull away
the leather helmet and stand,
a damp-haired boy surrounded
in the summer hay.
*Give him some tea, poor love*
I heard them say
as the metal chatter
of the guns fell
like lark song from above.

# WAR PAINT

The girl in Belsen thought she was dead,
until an English boy who'd never been
to France or Germany,
never asked to leave his Mum
and sisters back in Kirkby,
to run down lanes while someone
shot at him, threw bombs on his head,

came through a gate and gave the girl
in stinking rags who couldn't walk,
a dish of porridge, drink from a flask,
and a tube of lipstick red as blood,
glistening and perfumed.

# FIGHTING CHANCE

It was forbidden to scorn my mother
when she bowed her head to the Pope
blessing the crowd on television.

My father lost his faith
some time before he fell
out of a plane above Bayeux.

He lost it as his sister coughed
in the room above the kitchen,
where his father slept,
too tired to climb the stairs.

Though he'd fallen in the night
like Icarus and lived
the luck that made this so
was not respected, unlike faith.

# ASOSA

I think of you going to the edge of nowhere,
to the camp of a million homeless.
The roads are red dust
lined with dripping green trees
but then the desert, stretching to the river.

I hope you are safe as well as happy.
There's nothing I can do about either,
so far away and busy you cannot think of me
and shouldn't try.
We will visit next year,
that's one more thing for you to worry about.

Here people are driving home from work.
It's winter so their headlights flash
across the ceiling like searchlights
in war time, when the bombers came.
Where you are, out there in the middle of the world,
light comes and goes the same time every day,
slow dawn, no dusk, quick blindfold dark.

We send you books they cannot read,
but the pictures and turning the pages are enough.
They quieten, crowded together in the shade.
You give them pens, crayons, paper,
so the parents, bereft of all they had
except their children, can for a while
forget their caring and their failure.

If I could talk to you about all this
I'd sleep better these long nights.
When you and your friends ride back
along that red dust road,
leave before the sun goes down,
don't stop.

# SANDY PYLOS

The chameleon
ate the fly
that drank the sweat
of Telemachus
as he rode through reeds
from the Cow's Mouth.

*Where is my father?*
He asks the king
who says *Before I answer*
*you must bathe*
and calls his daughter
who takes the boy
helps him into
a low clay bath
sealed with painted
dolphins and blue waves
and with her fingers
presses salt and dust
from his pores
tips jugs of water
on his head then
lifts him by one armpit
to stand beside the tub
rubs scented oil
into his frame
takes a blade
peels a skim of oil
and skin from spine
sacrum sternum
belly breast
re-anoints him
with a lighter balm,

so he is ready
to hear Nestor say
*Odysseus*
*should have returned*
*ten years ago.*
*You are alone.*

# A MATTER OF COURSE

Look what life has done,
rounded our edges,
coloured in our black and white,
bowed our shoulders,
loosened our clothes.

What was anticipated
has run through our hands.
I caught some of it,
even the sun and sky today
are my portion.

The rest I was afraid of
or couldn't grip,
decisions lying on the mat
before the door was opened,
before the question was asked.

Sometimes I go back,
see my sandaled feet
in the shallows,
and when I turn
folded green hills,

a road winding up
between them,
which goes to places
I cannot name
but know.

# ALL THE NUMBERED YEARS

I see the number on the cover
and realise that diaries will be made
until the dates run out and the shop shuts.
Before then, on a day already
waiting to be printed,
I will have stopped choosing in December
an oracle for next year.

We don't know what will happen
but the diary does. There's plenty of time
and it's all arranged. A column a day,
a week on a desk, a year in a pocket.
In the unwritten page we will go
with our children to a small town
where there is a particular mountain
then we won't, though they might
and others will, again.

The question is what to do with this
stone in the road, locked door,
fall off the world that Columbus feared.
Though he found a bay, moored up,
rowed in with his friends,
waded ashore and then without
knowing or wanting to killed everyone.

# SOLSTICE

A magpie crackles on your roof
telling an old story and old true truth.
Your neighbours sit on chairs
for sale outside your door,
peer down the cellar, under beds.
The hall is piled with crocks,
your lease ran out, you are buried,
the sun is shining, no one's sad.

A bunch of spoons in an elastic band,
a box of china sold unseen.
Your kids have put a price
on every sideboard, frame, cup, knife.
A pocketful of cash for fifty years
in hardware shops, general stores,
Saturday afternoons on Wandsworth road.
Each bargain shoving last week's snip
to the back of the shelf.

Stained ceilings painted over,
I should know I've put ten coats on ours.
The house promiscuously doesn't care,
looks out the window for someone else
to open its gate and pay to enter.
Four long June days to clear the lot.
Thirty thousand ascents of the stairs.
I buy a spade you forgot you'd bought.

The letter box is nailed shut
to stop reminders that the future
is still alive from littering the mat.
Your son wants more than I will offer
for a copy of Our Mutual Friend,
to stack with other books piled up
as insulation against the cold
that walls of oak lath, plaster,
brick and render, cannot keep out.

# NEAR CLUN

I heard you lived
in a village off
the small main road
and went there on foot.
Left my car
by the crossroads,
walked down the lane
past cottages
cleaned up
to look like cottages,
smoke from chimneys,
ivy'd porches,
an ancient, empty church,
maintained by urgent
appeals for funds.
Even the vicar
only visits
once a month,
local agnostics
unlock the gate,
mow the graves,
decorate the altar
and switch on the organ
for visiting musicians.

I asked a gentleman
up a ladder
trimming privet
if he knew
where the poet lived.
He didn't but
when I said
you ran a bookshop
he knew the shop.
I gave up,
walked back

in November light,
brown leaves, mist.
Crossing streams
and pausing because
if you stop
above a river
where you stand is always
running away
beneath you
like the seconds
just gone and to come,
not there.

Drove to my mother
who did not know anything
except that she was alive
and defeated,
that I was there,
and would soon be gone.
I asked myself
as I left,
what's the point
of living in a
country village
if you don't
know everyone,
I thought
that was the idea?
You might as well
live where I do,
in a city street
where I know my
neighbours' names
but not all of them
and those
whose names I know
are strangers.

# HOUSE HUNTING

What happened to Mrs B
who lived in Beaufort street?
Offered us a place
and didn't take it back
when she first saw us,
out at heel, one case,
baby in a basket.
She kept faith
and handed us the key.

Then we wronged her,
ran away, erased
from the directory when
we turned the corner
in a hired van,
all four of us in front,
watching out for cops
while waiting to cross
at the junction
on Wandsworth road.

Beds, books, pots, guitars
packed in the back,
pulled up outside a terrace
with a purple door,
bare wires in the hall,
a roof of cracked
Welsh slate.

\*

When you asked,
*Do you want to die in this house?*
that was unexpected
as we were driving north
on the A3 at the time
and my answer,
*I'm going to live for ever,*
didn't help.

We've been here too long,
so we search down backstreets
in south coast suburbs,
anywhere the sea suddenly opens
its unforgiving horizon
and reassuring breath.

But if we'd moved ten times
since nineteen eighty
we'd still be on the A3,
wondering what to do
with the time we think
we have left.

## A STOP ON THE WAY

Instead of wondering
*Here or further on?*
turn into a lane
where signposts promise
quiet hamlets
settled in fields.

One offers 'St Mary's Church',
a Victorian tower on older walls,
and a pew labelled
'In memory of Maud,
 who loved this place'.

Summer heat but after rain
the grass and trees welcome it.
We sit awhile, long enough,
then drive back to the highway
that heads west over the hill,

the highest point round here.
Beyond it farms, rivers,
lanes and crossroads,
all the way to the coast
where we must go
together.

# I NEVER THOUGHT I'D LIVE ROUND HERE SO LONG

Roots beneath the clay,
hauling water through the slabs,
the tree across the road is at home.
I know each tree and gate,
the roof line level's change
where the builder stopped,
the almond blossoming on April 1st,
the empty kerbs of August.
From the cracks between each second
rise things I've seen and done
more present than where I am,
standing on the pavement.

The crescent moon and star
above the door on Falcon Road
I once went through
and was given a glass of water,
*La ilaha illa'llah.*
The masjid on Rue Mouffetard
that first time we tried to walk to Rome.
The scent of dust in a shadowed lane
outside Al-Karaouine.

I return through our gate
which someone a century ago
hung on a post that's been
replaced ten times.
These numbers don't add up
and if we left tomorrow for elsewhere,
I'd still only recognise the sky,
early morning air, sunset again,
leaving a mat of unread paper,
the key in an unread palm,
no forwarding address,
this knocker hammering on another life.

# HOLDING THE LINE

Her father was a sailor
who sought the shortest route.

Her seamstress mother
sewed a neat straight hem.

She fitted gyroscopes that made
torpedoes run a fast white line

and raised two kids
when that was done.

    \*

She knows time
to the minute.

When to rise,
when to eat,

when to go out.
If the gardener

is late
she is afraid.

The clock goes quiet
each afternoon.

She watches light
in the tree outside,

that as it fades
alerts the ticking

in each room to start
the habits of the night –

wash, dress, wine,
a narrow bed.

      *

She calls to say
*Don't feel you have to visit*

*this old woman.*
Her diary plans her fate,

she cannot read
her ticked off past

and walks quickly to
her next appointment.

# SOME ENCHANTED EVENING

I'd hear him before
he came round a corner,
hands in pockets.
On mountain paths
he called the dogs
with another note.

I learnt how
to use my lips,
and the thinner tone
made by making a reed
from the tongue's tip
against the mouth's roof.

Driving fast
so our dust
could not catch up
we piped show-tunes
to accompany the engine's
drone and silence.

\*

In the final place
he apologised,
said he wanted
to go back home.
The nurse wheeled him out,
washed and tidy,

told him he must try
to move and sip.
So with two of us
holding on
he leaned round the ward
once more

then lay back down,
eyes closed,
legs, hands
and lips together,
folding away,
clean as a whistle.

# AGAINST ENGLAND

Stopped at the lights I saw
a grey curled hair Jamaican
lean his bike against the fence,
to watch the cricket
on Sunday afternoon.

And recalled my father,
supporting the West Indies
always against England,
laughing as Marshall scuttled in
to fire invisible red comets
at Steele's straight bat.

Michael Holding long swooping
whisper across the grass,
to hurl a missile at
the waiting tall white man.

Andy Roberts, middleweight,
turning at the start of his run,
everyone in the ground aware
he wanted to hurt the batsman
as well as knock him out.

At Trent Bridge we saw
Hall and Griffith, quick, clean,
break bones and stumps.
Long days in the nets roughing up
Worrell, Sobers, Weekes,
so they wouldn't fear
Truman, Statham, Snow.

Dad sat there in the stand,
the sun lifting a perfume
of grass, old wood, beer.
Watched his compatriots go by,

caps, flannel trousers, jackets,
waistcoats, cigarettes at lip,
a blessed day of quiet and
spectacle away in the light from
the long loom and black pit.

Turned to me and said
he'd come to agree
his generation were done,
worn down, couldn't be bothered
about Vietnam, or books,
wanted their women in the kitchen,
scullery, bedroom, back yard.

I wish I'd never spoken
when I was young.
So easy to discount then
how they left fields, mines,
factory gates, their mothers' door,
to cross the sea, kill and die
for everyone still here –

me, waiting for the lights to change,
players and spectators spread out
across the field before the end of play,
with somewhere to go,
a week's work to do,

and the grey haired man
leaning against the fence
watching the cricket,
whose Dad maybe came
in '48 to bail us out
when we had shot our bolt.

# EASTERN AND ORIENTAL
*The E & O Hotel, Penang.*

When I went back to the E&O
the past was as usual present.
I met myself beneath a Casuarina
that shaded lizards
suspended on a wall
like seconds,
then my father buying kernels
from a man squatting over
a nest of paper cones.
As we walked to the hotel
I heard what he was saying
but not the words.

Odysseus poured blood
into a ditch in hell
to help his dead friends speak,
and my still pulsing life
filled corridors with familiars
who had stayed behind when I
went into the cloud of darkness
that spun down
from the ceiling fan
when we switched it off
and shut the door.

It's always the same at checkout.
You pay for time you've
already used, like laundry,
while the maid is in the room
cleaning ghosts away.

# VERONA

You wrote to say you were going
to Mantua in the Spring,
though first your doctor wished to try
the transfusion once again.

When I read this it was as if
you'd called from the front door,
*back in a minute*, then
hearing your steps hurry away.

But I'll put aside some days
next year to visit Mantua.
We could take the train
to Verona too, perhaps.

## THE WIND FORGETS, ALWAYS FORGETS
*George Seferis*

We've been here
only a few months.
In that time a woman

came to the door
to say
her husband
was dead,

cracked open
at the dinner table.

Also, a man
in the garden
heard his father

was sick,
then was told
he'd died
and quickly left

though the funeral
could never happen.

\*

The sun remembers
and returns each day
to the same places.

But the wind,
appearing suddenly
when you turn a corner,

hurtles past,
changing and forgetting
all it touches.

We open windows
to let it renew
our house,

sometimes omit
to close them
before it throws

a vase of flowers aside
on its way
to somewhere else.

# IN SURE AND CERTAIN HOPE

We walked
   from the church.
Thin daffodils shivered
   along the lane.
I thought we were
   going to the wake,
but we crammed inside
   flint walls,
tripping over stones
   blotched with lichen
like the bloom
   of mould
on an apple
   left in the bowl.

Green cloth
   concealing mud
where the digger's tracks
   had gripped
hung in the slot
   hiding slick
wet sides cut
   like a surgical incision.
In the water
   at the bottom
poached grey worms
   tried to swim.

Her nephews
   carried her in,
young bulls sweating
   under the weight,
feeling the load shift
   on their shoulder bones.

Wind blew the vicar's
    tippet round his neck
like a snake
    as he recited poetry
about what is true
    and what we'd like
to be true,
    small mortals cold
in early Spring.

A gust caught
    a woman's coat
as she leant over
    looking down,
felt herself falling,
    span round
and stepped away
    with almost a laugh,
saying she'd
    loved her sister
but didn't want
    to join her yet,
or their mother also
    down there, deeper.

Afterward she
    leant against the bar
picking at crisps
    with red-tipped fingers.
Glad that death,
    striking suddenly
through the house,
    had been cleared away,
sent back to its place
    hovering invisible
above the horizon
    day and night.

So we would not have to
    watch her change
we left her where
    we didn't want
to leave her,
    blocked in, clay bound,
alone, but then
    her soil-clogged eyes
appear at noon.
    It's better to burn
and be gone,
    a warm soul of dust
scattered in the air,
    like the first cut
of the year.

# GIVE US THIS DAY MARCH 29TH 2020

Blackthorn flowering along the track
then the sea, crossed by shadows,
like a lizard's eye, blinking.
The tide is coming in but
I can get out on the sand,
untrodden since we sold an hour
to buy a later twilight.
Now, in this time we bought,
the breeze has dropped
and Easter blossom hangs
in the hedge like a wreath.

# FORECASTING THE PRESENT

I notice it every time,
one hand stuck on FAIR
through winter, summer.

George III, M. Woller,
Vernier scale, detachable
hygrometer.

Silent moon face
in the corridor,
glanced at, tapped,

should blink
and elegantly explain
the weather in the window,

but the mercury,
once liquid in its
tall, thin tube,

is black and stuck,
insisting climate
does not change.

I'll get it fixed,
I like to know
what's happening,

turn the wheel
so one hand marks
where the level rests

beneath earth's tidal air,
full of swift, quicksilver
shoals this afternoon.

Tomorrow it will recall
where we were,
and its companion

tugged by a thread will say
if we slid down or
climbed up from yesterday.

# ALSO

I put a mirror on
                the table
and see my eyes
                looking
at my eyes also
                the window
behind me and
                through it
backward
                I see also
the moon
                also the moon
painted on
                a blue screen
I know is
                not there
although
                I can see it
I could see
                all the way
to Neptune
                if I could
the seer
                cannot see
the seeing
                the round world
flattens
                on the lens

# THE BRIDGE

Metal slats rattle,
the gorge drops away,
filled with gravity
and falling.

In the café
above the edge,
a thimbleful
of aromatic sand.

Then drive on
to where the road ends
and the trail
over the mountain starts.

Small houses hidden in trees
and vines down lanes,
geraniums growing
in an empty oil can
painted blue,

a white dust path
threading away uphill.
I stop in the shade
and turn the car to face
the way we came.

# LEAVING NOW

We said goodbye

to the path across the common,
that in summer was white and hard,
in winter brown and muddy,
so people walked on the grass
and the path got wider.
The cherry and almond trees
outside our windows that were
flowering when we first arrived.

Mr Patel who sent our
daily paper and sometimes didn't,
José who cycled to work
each night and slept all afternoon
if the builders let him.
Our holly tree that propped
the fence between us and
the old man who we heard
complain but never saw.

The 319 across the river's
slick grey snake, always
leaving the city for the sea
or speeding inland to escape.
The morning footsteps and
at 10 the cleaners talking
on their phones, unlocking doors.
The street where we lived,
that sometimes led to home.

When the trucks drove off
we got in our car and sat
by the kerb for a while.
The engine fired and as
we turned the corner
and said goodbye
all that changed to being
unchanged like the sea floor
far beneath the tide.

# JACOB

Some early morning
when you wake,
a ladder of light

up the wall
where the shutter
is still closed.

A bird,
maybe a dog far off,
and quiet waves.

What you hear
is the sun,
holding its breath.

# MIDWINTER INVITATION

Though the sun stands still and cold
darkness seems to lengthen, deepen,
despite being trimmed a fraction.
On a foggy morning, barometer rising,
almost invisible sparrows play in the wood
like small falling leaves that sing.
They don't mean to teach me but they do,
so I've hung a hotel on the shed for them
next spring, or sooner if snow comes.
In due course the sun will pause again,
next time overhead at noon,
and the busy team chasing
across the road will still be here,
living on scraps of dust and air.

# WHEN IT'S ALL SAID AND DONE

In the window
I saw the end of the world.
The sky was clear.

The end of the world?
I saw how we would end,
disappear.

We?
I mean humanity,
all of us.

All of us?
Not at once,
gradually.

Gradually?
Yes, million
after million.

And we'll
take the world with us?
Some of it.

How will it end?
This is how it will end.

The sky will be clear.
It will be daytime.
Nothing will happen.

It will all have happened.
The soft rind of the planet
will have been unpeeled.

Desert, mountains,
small creatures underground,
will not notice.

Two people
open a gate
and go into a garden.

The great tree
rises before them
hung with snakes and angels.

They do not know
which is which.

# DID YOU MAKE IT?

and did you make the
most of it and did
you make the most of
it and did you make
the most of it and
if you did it will
be gone for ever
just as if you'd done
nothing as if you'd
done nothing as if
you'd done nothing so
filling each hour with
new thoughts and acts
and lying on the ground
with eyes shut all day
and night are the same
but if your eyes are
open looking up at
night you will see
stars return and the
moon make and unmake
its round silver self
and by day the sun
if clouds allow will
walk across you dawn
to dusk it makes no
difference what we do
everything comes back
except for you.